I0019470

Why focus on Software Licence Management?

2

About the Book

Welcome to this book on *Why focus on Software Licence Management?* It is a Best Practice guide based on actual case studies in pioneering, designing and implementing software licence management frameworks across diverse organisations.

The guidelines in this book are mainly derived from a process of innovative ideas, their adoption and eventual optimisation. They can be tailored to suit individual requirements of each organisation and the changing times.

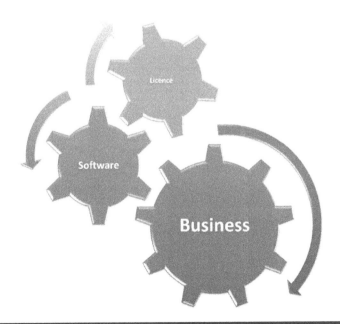

Why focus on Software Licence Management?

The picture above epitomises how Business, Software and Licences are intertwined with each other. Most businesses and organisations have huge investments in software and each software deployed or unused requires a valid licence. Each one of us is affected by licences since we use at least one software as part of Business or IT or as a customer. However, not much effort is put to manage these assets efficiently.

This book serves two major objectives. Foremost, it tries to understand, *"Why is it imperative to focus on software asset management?"* Secondly, it traces the key steps of the journey in implementing a robust framework based on actual case studies in different organisations. It will help you understand the importance of software licence management and provide concise guidelines to implement a framework that is apt for your organisation.

It will also help you realise that software assets are no longer liabilities once you have effective control on the total cost of ownership that guarantees a higher return on investments.

Author	R. Concessao
Copyright & Published by	iCS
Version	11
Dated	2011
Revised	2016

Limits of Liability & Disclaimer of Warranty

The author and publisher of this book and the associated materials have used their best efforts in preparing this material. The author and publisher make no representations or warranties with respect to the accuracy, applicability, fitness, or completeness of the contents of this material. They disclaim any warranties expressed or implied, merchantability, or fitness for any particular purpose. The author and publisher shall in no event be held liable for any loss or other damages, including but not limited to special, incidental, consequential, or other damages. If you have any doubts about anything, the advice of a competent professional should be sought. The names of software mentioned in this book are trademarks of their respective software providers and for the benefit of such companies with no intention of infringement of the trademark. Any unauthorised reprint or use of this material is prohibited.

Why focus on Software Licence Management?

About the Author

R. Concessao, is a Management Consultant at iCS.

My writings over the years are based on lessons learnt from nearly two decades of professional experience in IT and Management Consultancy based in Europe, Americas and Asia Pacific.

Predominantly, my experiences were in Fortune 100 and FTSE 100 companies operating in both global and regional models. My core competencies are in providing advisory services in Strategy and Leadership; Business Intelligence and Data Analytics; IT Service Management; Software Licence, Audit and Compliance Management; Scorecards and Dashboards; Web Content Development and Management; Training and Documentation.

My experience mainly stems from consulting, document management, educational, financial, healthcare, investment, logistics and supply chain, manufacturing, media, oil and gas, pharmaceutical, publication, public and services sectors.

Why focus on Software Licence Management?

This book is one among a few to be published and is a microcosm of my experiences in the area of Software Licensing. It took me more than a year to complete and I appreciate your interest in reading it.

Contents

Chapter 1: Introduction

A few years ago, I received a call from a Director in a leading multi-national company pointing to the need to overhaul their defunct Software Licence Management function. In the course of our conversation, I asked him, "What was his organisation's policy and direction"? He said, *"We need to move to a position where we can account for all our software, have a good command on our usage and project our demands accurately".* That pretty much summed up his requirements.

Subsequently, as part of an initial assessment, I interviewed a cross section of stakeholders from different facets of the organisation. These were some of their concerns and expectations. One of the major concerns of a Senior Leader was, to put it in his own words, *"We are not sure what exactly we own and how much we use?"* Yet another Senior Leader's expectations were succinct when he said, *"I would like to know exactly how many licences are required for all the software we have and the cost projections for next year".*

In another organisation, Global Purchasing department admitted that, *"We do not have all our contracts catalogued centrally. Those that are negotiated centrally have been filed here. But those that are negotiated by Business Units in operating countries or Project Teams independently fail to involve us and hence the contracts do not reach us".*

I also met a few SAP Technical Gurus in an organisation to understand the myriad nuances of SAP licences. They were extremely useful in providing me an insight into the SAP Licensing model. While congratulating me on taking an assignment with their organisation, one of them said *"Good luck, it will be a mission as SAP contractual paperwork is in a complete mess".* At that point, I thought *"maybe it was an overstatement and only time would tell".*

During my initial discussions with many organisations, Senior IT Executives told me, *"SAP requests us to provide annual software compliance reports on our licence usage and then requests for 'small considerations' i.e., extra payments, if they disagree with our measurements or suspect our licence usage is more than our entitlements based on ambiguous interpretations of the contracts".*

The above remarks are extraordinary. While the feedback highlighted their existing concerns, their expectations set the direction for us. They emphasise on *"Why the urgency and initiative to focus on Software Licence Management now?"* This is the core objective of this book.

In the course of the book, we will also go through the vision, strategy and model that were put in place to realise a robust Software Licence Management Framework in these organisations.

Chapter 2: What is Software Licence Management?

Software Licence Management is a business practice of managing and optimising licence usage through all stages of two lifecycles

- **Software Ownership Lifecycle** from the date of software purchase to the date it is decommissioned or reaches End of Service Life (EOSL) and

- **Employee or User Lifecycle** from the date an employee or user joins an organisation to the date an employee or user leaves the organisation

In other words, it is a practice where we account for all our software we own, understand the licences and types we have, utilise them optimally and comply with licence agreements signed with our software providers.

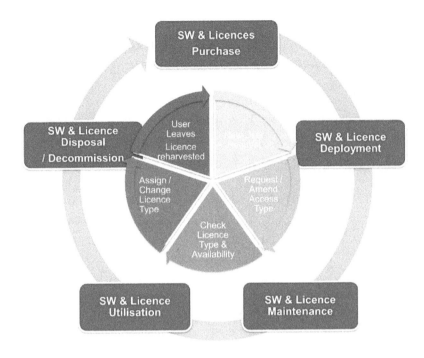

Figure 2.1: Software Ownership and Employee/User Life Cycles

Software Ownership Lifecycle

Software Ownership Lifecycle has five major stages. They are

1. **Purchase:** It is the first stage of the software ownership lifecycle. When software is purchased, it is important to have an unambiguous licence agreement which specifies exactly what we own,

how much we are allowed to utilise, how much we pay, any exceptions and conditions for renewal.

2. Deployment: At this stage, the Software is deployed, initial licences are assigned and accounted for.

3. Maintenance: This stage includes Licence or Maintenance & Support (M&S) renewals, additional purchase or returns and upgrades.

4. Utilisation: This stage includes monitoring the usage for over or under utilisation and ensures no exposure or wastage within reasonable limits.

5. Decommission: This is the last stage of the lifecycle where either the software has reached End of Service Life (EOSL) or it has to be decommissioned.

Employee or User Lifecycle

Employee or User Lifecycle has five stages. They are

1. **New User Request**: It is submitted either when an employee or user joins an organisation or moves into a new role. Normally one licence is allocated per user; but it could be per role for certain software.

2. **Request / Amend Access Type**: It is submitted when the role of an existing user changes and this in turn necessitates allocation of an appropriate access type.

3. **Check Licence Type and Availability**: The licence type and availability is checked based on the number of licences and the access type requested.

4. **Assign / Change Licence Type:** If the number and type of requested licence is available in stock, it is assigned to the user. Else, it is either assigned after optimisation or reclassification or additional purchase or it is rejected.

5. **User Leaves / Licence re-harvested**: When a user leaves or changes role, the software licence and its type is taken from the user and re-harvested to meet the next requirement.

Chapter 3: What are the different types of Software Licences?

Today, we have different types of software and correspondingly different types of licences. However, we can broadly classify them into three major types i.e., Simple Licences, Complex but Controllable Licences and Complex but Uncontrollable Licences.

Hopefully, these analogies may prove to be an eye opener to understand the concept of Software Licence Management and its major types. Let us start with

Simple Licences:

TV Licensing is probably the simplest form of Licensing. It is simple, because you pay a flat rate if you own a television in the UK and the rate is dependent on the television being coloured or black and white. We wish all software licences were as simple as this. Some of the licences belong to this category where you pay a licence fee per user or engine or server or CPU and for the edition used. These are tracked via a licence key. E.g., MS SQL Enterprise - Standard or Home Edition.

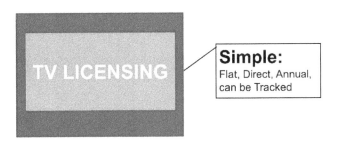

Figure 3.1: Simple Licences

Complex but Controllable Licences:

Imagine you want to buy Cable or Satellite TV service from one of the different service providers. Please note, that I am not promoting any of the satellite TV organisations or their products. Nor am I a celebrity or as influential as Oprah Winfrey to make a big difference.

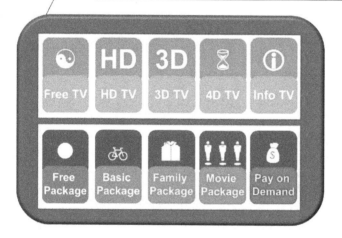

Figure 3.2: Complex but Controllable Licences

As evident from the picture above, the Satellite TV company offers different boxes like Free TV, HD TV, 3D TV, 4D TV and

Info TV each of which have a different charge depending on the option you choose. Once you have chosen the box, you next choose the type of package you require each costing a different charge per month. A family may decide to opt for HD TV and go for the family pack, movie pack and children's pack and get charged for all of them regardless of whether they watch all channels. We can have as many permutations and combinations.

Although a bit complex, you know exactly how much it costs beforehand regardless of whether you watch all the channels. If you prefer to watch Pay on Demand, you can opt and pay accordingly and it is perfectly within your control. Some of the software licences are slightly complex like this analogy but the costs can be controlled. E.g., In SAP, HR module licence combined with the Employee user type licences. In some software, there are multiple products or modules each having their own licences combined with 'Read Only' or 'Transactional' user type licences.

Complex and Uncontrollable Licences:

Let us now move on to an even more complicated model. Imagine you want to buy a Mobile Phone service. Firstly, you select the model of the phone and then the service plan, which provides fixed number of calls, texts and data. Again you can have as many permutations and combinations. However, the difference here is, if you exceed the plan in terms of the call limit or number of texts or amount of data downloaded, then you get charged extra.

However, there may be no mechanism in place to warn when you have reached your limit before the charges are levied. Some of the licences are complicated like this analogy. E.g., SAP user licences and QAS licences based on the amount of data downloaded or based on the number of clicks. In both examples, it is important that we track their usage to avoid financial exposure.

Complex and Uncontrollable
By Product Type and Service Plans
i.e., Calls, Texts, Data

Service Plan

Duration: 12 months

Calls: 100 minutes

Texts: 500 Texts

Data: 1GB

Figure 3.3: Complex but Uncontrollable Licences

Chapter 4: What are the different types of Software Licensing Models?

We have spoken about the analogies between everyday life scenarios and Software Licensing. Purchasing licences is akin to purchasing a house i.e., you have an initial Investment cost and an annual Maintenance and Support (M&S) costs.

Similarly, Software Licensing models have two types of charging mechanisms.

- **Investment Costs or Net Licence Fees**, charged once

- **Maintenance & Support Costs (M&S)** usually charged annually or for a defined term

Both serve as revenues for the software providers.

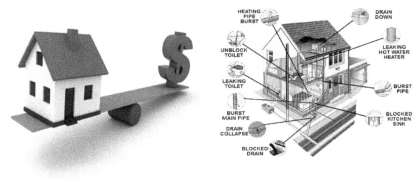

Investment / Net Licence Fees	Maintenance & Support Costs

Figure 4.1: Two Types of Costs

We used to have Licensing models primarily determined by physical attributes such as by number of users, by number of seats, by types of users, by number of engines or servers or CPUs or units or by number of databases or their clusters.

This is making a radical shift towards a usage based model that charges for licences by revenue, by number of clicks, by amount of data downloaded or a combination of the above. Hence, it requires a greater level of transparency through factual and unambiguous measurements on usage and entitlements.

The advance of technology and the advent of virtualisation, Software as a Service (SaaS) and Cloud Computing has changed the nature of the model and compounded Software Licence Management. We have different licence types for Enterprise Applications from different software providers. Not surprisingly, the list and the complexities keep growing day by day. Hence, the manifestation of the challenges faced by customers and their software providers.

Chapter 5: Why focus on Software Licence Management now?

We need to understand what really drives customers or organisations to focus on Software Licence Management now. Software Licence Management is governed mainly by a relationship between the Software Providers and their Customers. This relationship has its own challenges, risks and opportunities. They are influenced by a plethora of external and internal drivers at strategic, tactical and operational levels.

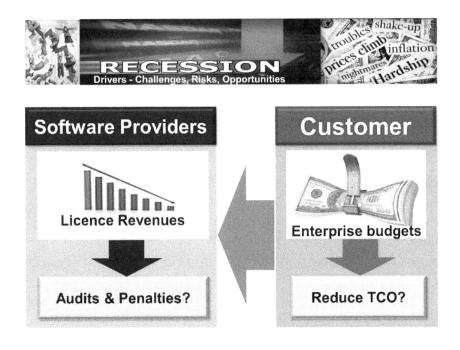

Figure 5.1: Drivers behind Software Licence Management

Why focus on Software Licence Management?

Today, we will focus on just two key drivers behind this initiative, one driven from a RISK perspective and the other from an OPPORTUNITY perspective.

In this day and age of austerity and a struggling economy, organisations are faced with frozen or shrinking budgets. It has put tremendous pressure on expenses and we are exploring avenues for cost savings by resisting the temptation to buy new licences. This in turn has initiated a vicious cycle in which the Software Providers are witnessing a decline in their revenues from new software licences and their annual Maintenance and Support (M&S) costs, which form their bread and butter.

Desperate times call for intelligent measures. Software Licence Management being an untapped domain in many organisations provides a perfect opportunity for the software providers to look for new revenue streams through increased surveillance on customers for piracy, infringement of their intellectual property rights and over utilisation of their licences. Software Providers have resorted to pursue costly and intrusive software audits which are akin to tax inspections.

The onus is always on the tax payer to pay the correct tax. If the Taxman suspects your tax dues, they will come down heavily on the defaulter. Similarly, a Software Provider has the right to audit at short notice and charge financial penalties if their customers are non-compliant, over utilise their licence entitlements and are financially exposed.

Remember

"The vendor is our friend if we under-utilise and over pay them; But a threat when we over utilise and under pay them"

As a customer, the threat of a software audit confronts the organisation with financial penalties running into thousands or millions of dollars while the senior executives like the CFO or CIO or CEO could face criminal prosecution, fines and unwarranted media attention since they are directly responsible for any breaches.

The question you need to ask is

Why focus on Software Licence Management?

- *Are you facing a RISK of a software audit from your software providers?, and more importantly*

- *Are you prepared for it?*

What do you think? How many of you think your company or organisation is facing a RISK of a software audit from your software providers?

In this cost challenged world, Software Licence Management being an untapped domain also provides an opportunity for organisations to optimise usage, pay for what is actually being used, and thereby reducing wastage and hence costs. Reducing the Investments or Net Licence fees on new licences and their associated annual Maintenance and Support (M&S) costs reduces all the direct and indirect costs associated with owning software. In other words, it reduces the total cost of ownership (TCO) of software.

The question you need to ask is

- *Is there an OPPORTUNITY to reduce TCO in response to tightening budgets?*

Chapter 6: Do you know your Baseline?

> **1.Are we facing a RISK of software audit?**
> • **If so, are we prepared?**
>
> **2.Is there an OPPORTUNITY to reduce TCO?**

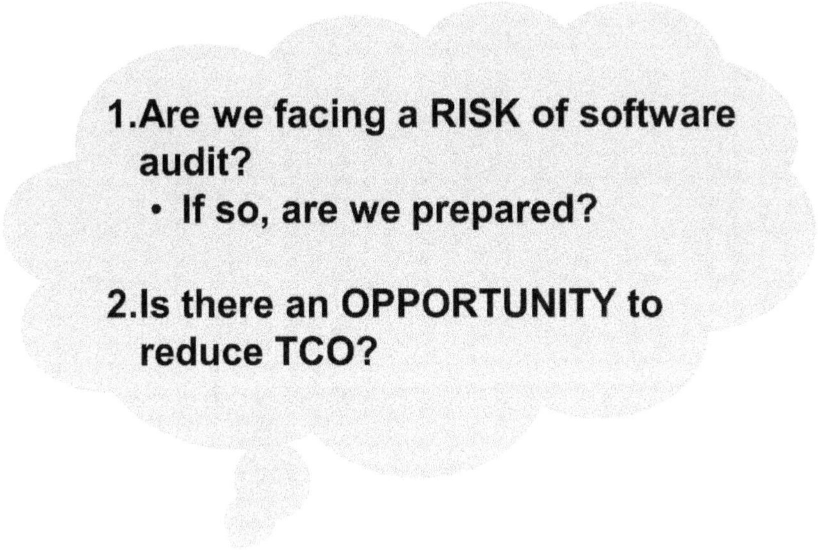

Figure 6.1: Do you know your baseline?

The two questions mentioned above can be better answered only if you know your baseline – i.e.,

1. *Who are your major software providers and how much do you pay them?*

2. *How many licences do you own for each software and how many do you really utilise? This includes over-usage and under-usage.*

3. *What is the financial exposure due to over-usage and wastage due to under-usage?*

Chapter 7: Who are your major Software Providers?

First, we need to know who your major software providers are and how much do you pay them. According to Gartner,

"Software Licensing costs are one of the major expenses borne by organisations. About 30% of our CAPEX and OPEX charges are related to software and their licences".

For the purpose of this book, we will go with our hypothetical organisation Rocorp Inc. Rocorp Inc. spent about $50m in software Investments and about $14m in annual Maintenance and Support (M&S) costs for selected enterprise software. These figures are based on research into licence agreements dating back over a decade and initial conversations with key stakeholders from different facets of the organisations, most notably Global Purchasing and Finance.

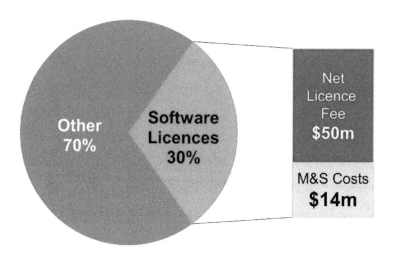

Figure 7.1: Capex and Opex Spend on Software

SAP ranks as our major software provider accounting for a whopping **80%** of investments or net licence fees while the remaining software providers are trailing behind.

Not surprisingly in the annual Maintenance and Support (M&S) costs pie, SAP ranks the first accounting for **71%** while the remaining software providers are trailing behind.

Investments or Net Licence Fees		
SAP	80%	$40m
Oracle	10%	$5m
Microsoft	8%	$4m
Others	3%	$1m
TOTAL	100%	$50m

M&S Costs		
SAP	71%	$10m
Oracle	14%	$2m
Microsoft	7.5%	$1m
Others	7.5%	$1m
TOTAL	100%	$14m

Figure 7.2: Breakdown of Costs by Investment vs. M&S

This answers the first of our questions in our quest to understand our baseline i.e., *"Who are your major software providers and how much do you pay them?"*

Chapter 8: Are you at RISK of a Software Audit?

In Rocorp Inc., since SAP forms the bulk of our spend both in terms of investment and annual Maintenance and Support (M&S) costs, we will be using SAP as a case study to check if we are at a RISK of a software audit and if we have an OPPORTUNITY to reduce our TCO.

We will go through two illustrations to check if we are at a **RISK** of a software audit from SAP – one based on SAP user type licences and the other based on SAP Engine type licences.

Example 1: RISK of financial exposure due to SAP user licences

Let us analyse the RISK of a financial exposure due to over utilisation of SAP user type licences. We calculated a financial exposure of $2m to 4m in this particular case study. This may vary from case to case depending on the contract and its terms and conditions.

How did we arrive at this value?

Over-usage of Licences
SAP Risk: Total exposure of $2m to $4m

Figure 8.1: Financial Exposure due to over utilisation

We need to answer the second question to understand our baseline, *"How many SAP licences do we own and how many of it do we actually utilise?"*

Let us start with a view at 30,000 feet level. The total number of SAP user type licences owned is 15,000. The HR headcount is 16,000. Since, each employee has access to HR portal and is a SAP user, each employee accounts for 1 SAP licence. But, the two numbers don't match. Clearly the RAG status in red demonstrates over-utilisation and non-compliance. However, SAP licensing is not that simple and straightforward.

SAP Licences Purchased	15,000
Head count (SAP users)	16,000

Figure 8.2: Headcount vs. Number of SAP Licences

Let us now go a level deeper at about 20,000 feet and check our utilisation across each of these user licence types. As you may be aware, we have different user licence types from Category II to Category V and beyond.

The main categories are

Category II – mySAP Professional

Category III – mySAP Limited Professional

Category IV – mySAP Employee

Category V – mySAP Developer

Category II (mySAP Professional) is the most expensive and Category IV (mySAP Employee) is the least expensive. If you check the table and the RAG status in *Figure 8.3*, we can see that we are under-utilising our Category II and III licences but over-utilising our Category IV and V licences. Hence, the total user licences used (16,000) is more than the total user licences purchased (15.000). Again, confirming that we are over-utilising our SAP user type licences and hence non-compliant.

But the question is, *"What is the financial exposure due to over-utilisation and wastage due to under-utilisation"?* This is the third question to understand our baseline.

User Type	II	III	IV	V	Total
Purchased	8,000	6,000	1,000	0	15,000
Used	7,000	5,000	4,000	100	16,100

Figure 8.3: Number of SAP Licences Used vs. Purchased

We will have to delve a bit deeper to understand the financial exposure in our next table. As evident from the table in *Figure 8.4*, we can observe a 1:1 mapping between the usage table and the costs table. Clearly we have financial wastage in Category II and III licences but financial exposure in Category IV and V licences which in total ranges from $2m to $4m; the lowest price taking actual list price and applying the 50% discount that SAP offered at the time of purchase and the highest is without the 50% discount.

User Type	II	III	IV	V	Total
Purchased ($m)	22	12	1	0	35
Used ($m)	17	10	2	1	30

Figure 8.4: Cost of SAP Licences Used vs. Purchased

Please note, the Oracle database licence costs of 14% and the annual Maintenance and Support (M&S) support costs of approximately 25% of the investment amount for the number of years exposed would be extra.

Although, we are in the red by over-utilising Category IV and V licences, the total value of the licences used is in green since the gross value of the licences used is less than the gross value of the licences purchased by about $5m.

This is a contradiction and unacceptable in normal software licence parlance.

Why is it unacceptable?

Take an example of a mobile phone plan from a mobile company. If you had a plan with 100 minutes of talk time and 200 texts and you exceeded your talk time but never used the texts. You cannot go back to your mobile service provider and request them not to charge you extra for the talk time exceeded or request them to offset the value of the unused texts to pay for the excess talk time used.

Similarly, we cannot request SAP for a refund for not utilising Category II and III licences optimally or request them to offset the surplus value in Category II and III licences with the shortage in Category IV and V licences.

However, we have an exception. A **Flexible Clause** in the latest **Exhibit** states that *"The total value of the licences used should not exceed the total value of licences purchased"*. Since the total value of the licences used ($30m) is less than the total value of the licences purchased ($35m), we are compliant and not financially exposed.

However, we need to be vigilant and ensure that we are below this threshold until the expiry of the flexible clause.

In the long term, we also need to take some proactive action before the expiry date and either,

- Extend the clause or

- Give SAP our exact requirements in licence numbers by category and buy additional Category IV and V user licences or

- Exchange excess user licences in Category II and III for additional Category IV and V licences or think of other alternatives.

The flexible clause is subject to SAP's sole discretion and is normally extended if the organisation or customer has made further investments through additional SAP user or engine or other licences or made additional payments to extend the clause.

Flexible Clause in Exhibit states that

"Value of licences used should not exceed total of gross licence fees of licences purchased".

Figure 8.5: SAP Flexible Clause

Have you noticed an anomaly?

If you look closely, the total number of user type licences used (16,100) is more than the headcount (16,000). If each employee/user counts as one SAP licence, then this is an anomaly. There are many factors behind this anomaly.

One of the factors is duplication, where some users have two or more SAP licences since they have multiple email addresses and the unique ID is based on email address.

This can be resolved through regular user audits or sanity checks every quarter and by reclassifying user licences as part of the compliance and optimisation drive.

Example 2: RISK of financial exposure due to SAP Engine licences

Let us analyse the RISK of a financial exposure due to over utilisation of SAP Engine licence by revenue. We calculated a financial exposure of $1 to $2m in this particular case study. This may vary from case to case depending on the contract and its terms and conditions.

How did we arrive at this value?

Software Engine licence by Annual Revenue
SAP Risk: Total exposure of $1m to $2m

Figure 8.6: Financial Exposure due to SAP Engine Licence

In the table in *Figure 8.7*, we can see that the licence fee applicable for revenue up to $2b is $1m. We are covered for SAP investment/net licence fee up to this band and had paid for it. We have also been paying our annual Maintenance and Support (M&S) costs of approximately 25% on this investment. However, in our example, the revenues have surpassed this band many years ago and based on annual figures in 2011 stood at $8b. Clearly, this implies we are non-compliant.

By Revenue Type	Revenue	Licence Fee
Purchased (Exhibit)	Up to $2b	$1m
SAP Licence Rate	$2b to $10b	$2m
Actual 2011	$8b	$1m to $2m

Figure 8.7: SAP Engine Licence Fee by Revenue

What is the financial exposure due to non-compliance?

According to SAP licence rates applicable, the licence fee for the revenue band from $2b to $10b in revenue is $2m. Hence our estimate of the financial exposure is from a minimum of $1m to $2m, the lowest price taking actual list price and applying 50% discount that SAP offered and the highest is without the 50% discount.

Please note, the Oracle database licence costs of 14% and the annual Maintenance and Support (M&S) costs of approximately 25% of the investment amount for the number of years exposed would be extra.

In the above example, the assumption is that the total revenue of $8b is generated through SAP systems. But, the reality could be that the organisation would have had revenue streams generated through other Enterprise applications or a combination of SAP and these applications. It is very important to ascertain the exact revenue generated through SAP based on volume of key transactions and the financial generated.

What are Software Licence Penalties?

We know that any outstanding tax attracts penalties from the taxman. Similarly, software providers will levy penalties on financial exposures after an audit.

Penalties
• **8-12 times audit fees ($150 to $2,000)**
• **$30k to $150k for each missing evidence or accidental or deliberate violation**

Figure 8.8: Range of Penalties

While our intention is not to sound **alarmist**, we need to be cognizant that the penalties are 8-12 times the audit fees. The audit fees ranged from $150-2000 per desk in 2011. The penalties range from $30-150k for each missing evidence or accidental or deliberate violations.

Is the writing on the wall? How many of you now think you are at a RISK of a software audit?

Certainly, there is no room for business as usual and you need to get your act together to ensure you are prepared for software audits from software providers. This is quintessential for software with high spends like SAP or software with high risk of an audit or a combination of both.

Similarly, we can identify other risks, gaps and exceptions that could potentially expose organisations financially.

Chapter 9: Is there OPPORTUNITY to reduce TCO and improve ROI?

You may come across these terms of consolidation and optimisation quite often and may wonder, *"How much do they really translate into cost savings"?*

Let us go through two illustrations to ascertain the cost savings – one worked out and the other a potential opportunity for you to take away and think about.

Example 1: OPPORTUNITY to optimise Category II licences

Let us take an example to illustrate an opportunity to optimise Category II (mySAP Professional Licences) in response to demands from a project. In Rocorp Inc., a Project Team had a demand proposal for 3000 new Category II type of user licences costing **$9m**. Our normal tendency would have been to go to SAP or the reseller and buy new licences.

However, through consolidation, optimisation, reclassification and re-harvesting of licences, the demand for new licences was brought down to 1000 users costing just **$3m.** This resulted in a cost savings of **$6m** or **67%** in investments alone.

Category II Licence	Users	Cost	Savings
Initial Demand	3,000	$9m	0
After Optimisation	1,000	$3m	$6m 67%

Figure 9.1: Costs Savings due to Optimisation

Where did the savings come from?

Of the $6m (67%) in cost savings,

1. Reclassification of licences accounted for $4.5m or 75%

2. Removal of dormant or unused licences accounted for $0.9m or 15%

3. Removal of multiple username accounts accounted for $0.6m or 10%

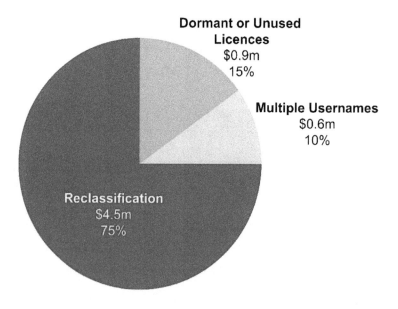

Figure 9.2: Cost Saving Initiatives

On average the cost savings range between 40-50% through consolidation and optimisation.

Typical Cost Savings through Optimisation

a. 60-90% cost savings is achieved for each re-classified licence type. Reclassification is the process of assigning the appropriate licence type to a SAP user based on multiple factors such as the highest role they perform, the number of transactions they use, the type of module(s) they use.

For example, let us take the graph below in *Figure 9.3* to depict the different categories or types of SAP licences and their costs. Please note these costs are to illustrate a point and need not necessarily be the actual costs of the licences.

Cost of SAP User Licences

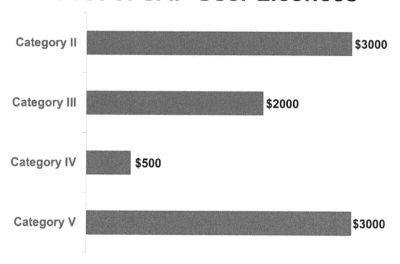

Figure 9.3: Cost of SAP Licences

- The graph shows the comparative cost of each of these user type licences from Categories II to V. Simplistically, downgrading a Category II to III user licence will reduce the cost by approximately 33% since the value of Cat III licence ($2000) is about 67% of Category II licence ($3000).

- Similarly downgrading Category II to IV user licence will reduce the cost by approximately 83% since the value of Category IV licence ($500) is about 17% of the Category II licence ($3000).

- Similarly, downgrading Category III to Cat IV user licence will reduce the cost by 75% since the value of the Category IV licence ($500) is 25% of the Category III licence ($2000)

b.   100% cost savings is achieved on deletion of each dormant account or unused licences.

   • These are licences of users who have left the organisation or do not use SAP anymore. Deleting these result in 100% cost savings each.

c.   100% cost savings is achieved on deletion of multiple username accounts of each unique user.

   • E.g., If Tom has two SAP licences i.e., Categories II and IV allocated since he has two email addresses or due to incorrect email addresses, one of them can be deleted resulting in 100% cost savings in that category.

In the example above, we have only mentioned savings of approximately $6m in investments or net licence fees. The savings on associated annual Maintenance and Support (M&S) costs is approximately $1.5m taking the total savings to approximately $7.5m in the first year of optimisation.

Example 2: OPPORTUNITY to reduce TCO by leveraging direct relationships

Let us take an example to illustrate an opportunity to reduce TCO by paying for Oracle database licences directly to Oracle rather than through SAP.

SAP Licence Costs	
Net Licence Fees	**M&S Costs**
$40m	$10m

SAP	Oracle DB	SAP	Oracle DB
$34.4m	$5.6m	$8.6m	$1.4m

Figure 9.4: Cost Savings through Direct Contracts

In this example, an organisation spent **$40m** on SAP Investments or Net Licence fees and **$10m** on annual Maintenance and Support (M&S) costs. Please note that **14%** of these costs are for Oracle DB licences and are paid to SAP instead of Oracle. This accounts for **$5.6m** in Investments or Net Licence fees and **$1.4m** in annual Maintenance and Support (M&S) costs. Historically, the organisation had also invested $20m with Oracle Business Suite products through net licence fees.

The question we need to ask is *"Is there an OPPORTUNITY to explore synergies to reduce the Maintenance and Support (M&S) costs by engaging directly with Oracle at a global level"?*

Example 3: OPPORTUNITY to reduce costs using tools

The two examples in *Chapter 9* show the cost savings through optimisation initiatives. If these are the cost savings and cost avoidance we can achieve by manually auditing, monitoring and analysing usage, imagine the efficacy of automating it through the use of auditing and monitoring tools which are available in the market.

We can achieve **70-90%** in cost savings by avoiding unnecessary wastage of resources through automated auditing and monitoring tools that serve both SAP and non-SAP software.

The comparative costs and efforts involved in auditing using an audit tool vs. manual method are shown below. The cost over 3 years of a tool is approximately $100k and the effort it takes to extract data, manipulate it, analyse it and generate reports is 1 to 3 hours depending on the system it accesses.

Compare this with the three-year cost of three FTEs at 150 days p.a. costing about $600k and effort of approximately 200 working hours to deliver the audit reports manually. The tool will also expedite the routine process of data extraction, manipulation and analysis and reduce human errors. This will enable the organisation to focus on identifying risks and mitigate them and exploring opportunities to reduce TCO.

To put this in perspective, if in an organisation,

1. Total investments in software assets was $50m,

2. These software assets generated an annual revenue of nearly $8b and

3. The cost avoidance and savings achieved using the manual software licence optimisation process so far was $20m,

the total cost of auditing and monitoring tool of $100k over three years is negligible.

The question you need to ask yourselves is, while you have a full-fledged security team and tools to take care of your physical assets like buildings, products and employee cars, do you have sufficient people and tools to look after your software estate with a value that is many fold more?

This completes the CORE section of the book by answering

"Why the urgency and initiative to focus on Software Licence Management now?"

Chapter 10: What is our vision?

We were invited by different organisations to help with Software Licence Management for different reasons. Some were driven by the threat of a software audit; some were driven by the ever increasing software costs and the rest out of their own volition for a leaner and efficient software licence management.

In one major organisation, we had put together a business case to answer the question, *"Why we need to focus on Software Licence Management?"* However, the Director came to me and asked, *"What was our next course of action?"* How do we carry forward this initiative and go about achieving its objectives?

The two major drivers behind this initiative i.e., the RISK of a software audit and the OPPORTUNITY to reduce TCO that we highlighted earlier in the CORE section of this book lead us beautifully into the four-point vision i.e., to achieve operational and compliance readiness.

The four-point vision was to

1. *Be prepared for a software audit*

2. *Provide business value to your value chain partners by reducing TCO through consolidation and optimisation*

3. *Plan effectively to meet new and future demands and*

4. *Transform your relationship with major Software Providers into a partnership based on "transparency", trust and mutual benefit.*

We have reviewed the first two points of the vision in the CORE section of this book.

The third point is about assessment of new and future demands and plan allocation of licences effectively. Some demands can be met by optimisation of existing licences as covered in *Chapter 9*. Any excess in demand will have to be met through the software procurement process.

You may have noticed that we sneakily brought in a fourth point into our vision and may question –

Why do we need to transform the relationship with our major software providers into a partnership?

Chapter 11: Why transform the relationship with our major software providers into a partnership?

In the CORE section of this book, we learnt that Software Licence Management is governed by a relationship between the software providers and their customers. This relationship is under severe strain due to many factors.

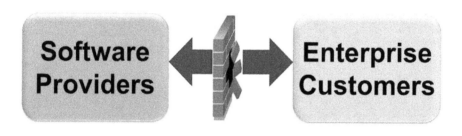

Figure 11.1: Relationship between Software Providers and their Customers

What are the fundamental factors that strain the relationship?

The fundamental factors that contribute to the strain in relationship are

1. The threat of a software audit by software providers. Software providers have started to demand **transparency or visibility into customer compliance.**

   E.g., SAP demands to provide annual software compliance reports on licence usage which are similar to self-assessment in taxation. As customers, we are unable to account for all our inventory, view all our entitlements, project our demands and costs accurately, measure for compliance on our own due to lack of standard tools and a mismatch in our measurements with those of the software provider. Customers have differences in interpretation with the software provider on measurements, entitlements and ambiguous contracts. This causes a strain on the relationship between the software providers and customers.

2. Software providers are under increasing pressure from customers to provide licence management or audit tools to generate software compliance reports. We are

also demanding software providers to be transparent and simplify their baffling measurement and charging mechanism. This again causes a strain on the relationship between the software providers and customers.

3. The ever changing technology and business trends are further complicating Licensing models.

- We used to have Licensing models primarily determined by physical attributes like number of users, number of seats, types of users, number of engines or servers or CPUs or units or number of databases or their clusters.

- This made a radical shift towards a usage based model that charges for licences by revenue, by number of clicks, by amount of data downloaded or a combination of the above. Hence, it requires a greater level of transparency through factual and unambiguous measurements on usage and entitlements.

- The advance of technology and the advent of virtualisation, Software as a Service (SaaS) which is basically renting software (e.g., BigMachines, SalesForce.com) and Cloud Computing has changed the nature of the model and compounded Software Licence Management.

- The change in business models through the use of offshoring, near-shoring and remote outsourcing has re-defined software licence management practices.

Hence, there is a mismatch between yesterday's contracts and today's realities. This causes a strain on the relationship between the software provider and customer. It is increasingly felt that a relationship based on "transparency", trust and mutual benefit will be a win-win situation for both the customer and the software provider and transform the relationship into a mutually beneficial partnership.

What are the advantages of a mutually beneficial relationship?

1. As a customer, it gives you the flexibility to renegotiate contracts to adapt to the changing business and technology needs. It will also avoid the risk of software audits and possibly remove the need for software compliance reporting.

2. For the software provider, it guarantees a regular cash flow and a long term and satisfied customer.

This clarifies the fourth point of our vision mentioned earlier i.e., *"Transform your relationship with major Software Providers into a partnership based on 'transparency', trust and mutual benefit"*.

Chapter 12: What is the Strategy and Roadmap?

An approach with a clear vision requires a clear cut strategy to realise the Software Licence Management Framework. Before we embark on any ambitious project or programme, it would be useful to know *"Where are we today"?* and *"Where do we want to go"?* This will help us determine the strategy and roadmap to achieve our objectives.

We developed a theory of strategic planning and put together a strategy which consists of three major stages i.e., Organise, Analyse and Mobilise, in that sequence.

Stage 1 - ORGANISE

As you can see from the first picture on the left of *Figure 12.1*, we are in a constant state of fire-fighting since our software assets and documents are all over the place.

The objective is to first ORGANISE ourselves and find all software assets, Proof of Purchase (PoP) Collaterals and licence agreements and store them in a central repository as exemplified in the picture to our right. This will help us review, analyse and check for any ambiguity or gaps in the contracts and address them.

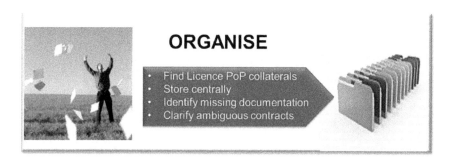

Figure 12.1: Stage 1 - Organise

For example, in some organisations,

1. We found incorrect Exhibits in their SAP contracts until they embarrassingly received the correct one from SAP.

2. We came across duplicate or extra software licences purchased directly from the software company and those purchased through a third party software dealer.

3. We noticed difference in user licence counts between the actual number from the business versus the higher number from licence agreements. The organisation was paying Maintenance and Support (M&S) costs on the higher number from licence agreements.

Stage 2 - ANALYSE

The picture on the left of *Figure 12.2* shows two groups of people dealing separately with the same software provider without any background information due to the lack of a central governance mechanism, dashboards and metrics.

The objective is to ANALYSE by understanding our current capacity, measure our utilisation through unambiguous dashboards and metrics, accurately project demands, consolidate our requirements and negotiate centrally with software providers to enable us to get discounts on bulk purchases as implied by the picture on the right in *Figure 12.2*.

This will help us pass on the discounts to our value chain partners. It will also help us make informed decisions, identify risks and mitigate them proactively and explore opportunities for cost savings and optimisation. We have seen evidence of these risks and opportunities with SAP licences in *Chapter 8 – Are you at a Risk of a software audit?*

Figure 12.2: Stage 2 - Analyse

Stage 3 - MOBILISE People, Processes and Tools

The picture on the left in *Figure 12.3* shows a confused man amidst pieces of scattered jigsaw puzzles, probably a Licence Manager or Software Asset Manager.

The objective is to MOBILISE by bringing together all disjointed entities i.e., people, data, processes and any tools or lack of it to form a meaningful framework as shown by the picture on the right in *Figure 12.3*.

It will also transform our relationship internally with our value chain partners and with our major software providers into a *partnership built on "transparency", trust and mutual benefit.*

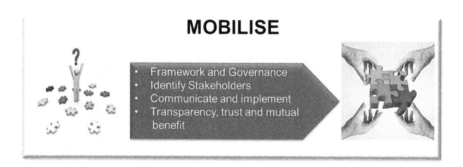

Figure 12.3: Stage 3 - Mobilise

To over-simplify, our STRATEGY to build the Software Licence Management Framework is to ORGANISE, ANALYSE and MOBILISE. The same strategy holds good to face a software audit but in a targeted approach and a quicker timeframe.

Chapter 13: What is Software Licence Optimisation Maturity Model?

To execute our strategy and roadmap, we need a mechanism to measure the progress within our organisation and use it as a benchmark for comparison between organisations.

What better way to measure ourselves than define an Optimisation Maturity Model as displayed in *Figure 13.1* with a starting point and a set of structured levels, like a staircase.

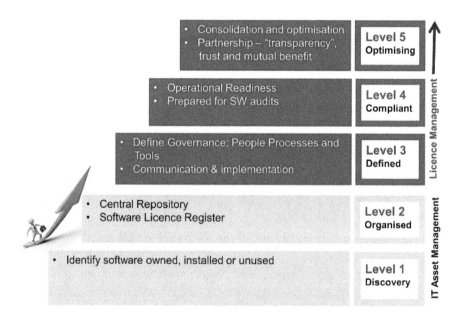

Figure 13.1: Optimisation Maturity Model

Each structure defines key process areas for improvement to achieve the desired goals in a defined timeframe, and establishes common features and key practices to implement the framework. There are 5 levels in total and let us start with Level 1.

Level 1 – Discovery Stage

It is the starting point to identify all software owned in your estate whether they are installed or unused. In some organisations, our scope was limited to "Enterprise software" within the remit of the Licence Management Team and used widely across the organisation. In one such organisation, we identified more than 25 software from over 15 software providers with more than 25 licence types and the list kept growing.

Level 2 – Organised Stage

In this stage, we shortlist all Software in scope and build a central repository containing all Proof of Purchase (PoP) collaterals i.e., licence agreements, contracts, exhibits, schedules, POs, invoices, credit notes etc. We also build a Software Licence Register (SLR), which is a database containing essential information on all software and their licences similar to a CMDB. Sometimes it is referred to as Software Asset Register. At this stage, you should be able to account for all your software and their Proof of Purchase (PoP) collaterals.

Level 3 – Defined Stage

In this stage, we have people and tools identified and processes defined, documented, communicated and implemented. The Governance model is defined to improve communication channels internally within an organisation and externally with the software providers. During this stage, all key stakeholders and tools are identified and the roles & responsibilities, processes and guidelines are defined.

Level 4 – Compliant Stage

At this stage, we are in a strong operational readiness position to maintain licence renewals automatically in advance, face any potential software audits and reviews. The contract monitoring mechanism and compliance checks are in place in terms of licence utilisation and financial exposure. We develop dashboards, metrics and reports on usage compliance, financial exposure and financials and have the ability to project demands and costs accurately.

Level 5 – Optimising Stage

At this stage, we manage to consolidate and optimise software, its licences and their vendors. We are able to ensure

- We do not have duplicate software unless required for contingency;

- We do not have duplicate or under-utilised licences unless we need the bandwidth for growth, and

- We have a centralised and consolidated software licence purchasing process providing for a central licence pool instead of piece meal approach among different operating countries.

- We are also in a position to transform our relationship with our major software providers into a partnership built on "transparency", trust and mutual benefit.

This is a continual improvement stage and will be on-going.

*The first two levels are coloured in beige and reflect the **IT Asset Management stage**. The next three levels in dark red reflect the **Licence Management stage**.*

Chapter 14: What are the foundations of Software Licence Management Framework?

The two key deliverables that form the foundation or bed-rock of Software Licence Management framework are

- Central Software Licence Repository and

- Software Licence Register

The other deliverables such as risk register, dashboards and metrics - usage and compliance reports, financial exposure reports, demand and cost projections and financials are covered later.

First Key Deliverable - Central Software Licence Repository

It is a key deliverable of *Level 2 - 'Organised' stage* of the Licence Optimisation Maturity Model covered in *Chapter 13*.

It serves as a single point of electronic documentation for all stakeholders who have access to it and stores the **soft copies** of all Proof of Purchase (PoP) Collaterals such as Contracts, Agreements, Exhibits, Schedules, Invoices, POs, Credit Notes.

It would be beneficial to push the envelope and go a step further to create Summary Files. The Summary files, provide a quick insight into the software licence details instead of surfing through innumerable pages of the contracts. The Summary files are produced after reading 1000s of pages of licence documentation and extracting critical data mainly related to costs i.e., Net Licence fees/Investments and Maintenance and Support (M&S) costs and any special clauses.

The **physical copies** of the documentation are also catalogued and maintained by Licence Management Team and Global Purchasing.

It is a massive exercise depending on the number of software providers and their respective number of exhibits, contracts, agreements and amendments.

Second Key Deliverable - Software Licence Register

It is a key deliverable of *Level 2 - 'Organised'* stage of the Licence Optimisation Maturity Model covered in *Chapter 13*. Sometimes, it is referred to as Software Asset register (SAR).

The Software Licence Register (SLR) is a database containing

1. Details of a software product – version, utility

2. Details of its licences - types, their numbers, validity term, purchase and renewal dates

3. Maintenance and Support (M&S) details – M&S availability, renewal dates and any special clauses

4. Contact details of software providers and the customer organisation

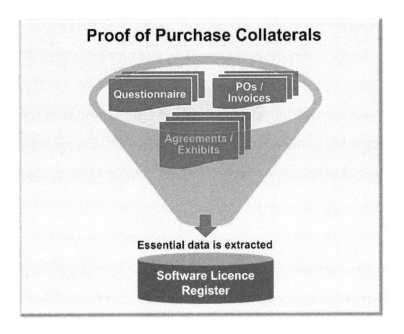

Figure 14.1: Software Licence Register

Input: The main input is the SLR Questionnaire sent to key application and service owners. The Proof of Purchase (PoP) collaterals like Licence Agreements, Maintenance & Support (M&S) Agreements, Exhibits, Schedules, POs, Invoices, Credit Notes and other documents from key stakeholders from IT Management, Application Teams, Finance, Global Purchasing and Service Delivery are collected, reviewed, analysed, summarised and critical data is extracted.

Output: The extracted data is then put in a structured database and forms the basis of the SLR.

Utility: The SLR is essentially like a CMDB and is accessible by all the key stakeholders i.e., Business, IT Management, Licence Management Team, Global Purchasing and Legal Team.

It provides stakeholders with a glimpse of all the software we have in our inventory, their versions, utility of the software (ecommerce, application, servlet, database, search engine); the licence type (user, server, database, transaction); term (perpetual, annual or a fixed term) and numbers purchased. If any Business Unit or Operating Country has a requirement for a particular software or its additional licences, they can check it directly on the SLR for both availability of the software and any spare licences.

The SLR also has licence purchase and renewal dates, Maintenance and Support (M&S) details including the term and its renewal dates and any special clauses. This is useful to ensure that they raise the POs in advance at the beginning of the year to facilitate automatic Maintenance and Support

(M&S) / licence renewals which are a major grievance of most software providers.

The SLR also has contact details of all software providers and key contacts within a customer organisation. This ensures good supplier relationship management and improves the ability to deal with technical or operational queries.

What are the other deliverables?

Some of the other deliverables such as risk register, dashboards and metrics, usage and compliance reports, financial exposure reports, demand and cost projections and financials are highlighted below. The detailed processes are not covered in this book.

Risk Register

A Risk Register is a central repository with a list of gaps, issues and opportunities identified by an organisation. Each risk record includes information such as risk probability, impact, mitigation, risk owner and so on. The gaps and issues are addressed based on the level of impact. The table below in *Figure 14.2* is an example of a Risk Register.

#	Type (Issue/ Risk / Opportunity)	Title	Description	Owner	Impact	Mitigation	Cost of Mitigation	Status
1	Risk	Audit Tool	Lack of licence audit and monitoring tool for SAP and non-SAP software	ABC	M	Buy Licence Tool	$106k	Business case presented

Figure 14.2: Risk Register

Some of the examples of gaps and issues include missing Proof of Purchase collaterals, pending Maintenance and Support (M&S) payments, delays in licence renewals and over usage of licences compared to entitlements.

Some of the opportunities include identification of duplicate software purchases from multiple sources, multiple software with similar functionality and lack of an early annual PO generation process to cover software licence renewals and Maintenance and Support (M&S) costs. These are managed at the Operational Level and if necessary escalated to the Tactical Level of the governance model discussed in *Chapter 15*.

Usage and Compliance Reports

Usage and Compliance Reports give you a detailed picture about the licence compliance status i.e., if a software is Compliant, Over Licenced or Under Licenced. They also provide a status of those licences that have to be renewed soon. If a tool is used to generate reports, you can configure alerts to remind

- If usage numbers are reaching licence threshold or breaching entitlements and
-
- If a software is being used after its licence has expired

The graphs below in *Figures 14.3 and 14.4* are some examples of Usage and Compliance Reports.

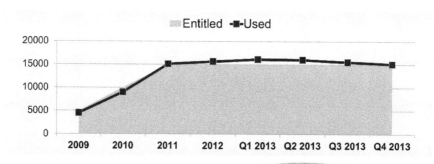

Effective Licensing Position - SAP Cat II to V Licences

SAP (Cat II to V) Licences	2009	2010	2011	2012	Q1 2013	Q2 2013	Q3 2013	Q4 2013
Entitlement	5000	10000	15000	15000	15000	15000	15000	15000
Used	4500	9000	15100	15600	16100	16000	15500	15100
Variance = Entitlement - Used	500	1000	-100	-600	-1100	-1000	-500	-100

Figure 14.3: Usage and Compliance Report

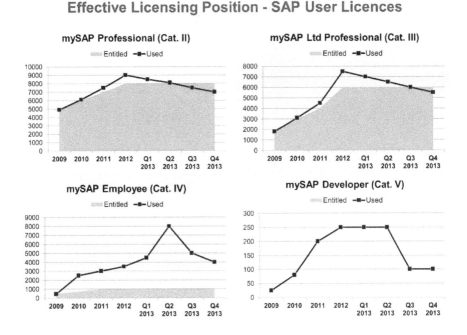

Figure 14.4: Usage and Compliance Report

Financial Exposure Reports

Some licence usage and compliance reports are not just based on usage numbers. They are also based on the financial value of licences used. This situation applies mostly when there are different categories of licences for a software.

For example, SAP has different categories like

Category II – mySAP Professional Licence,

Category III – mySAP Limited Professional Licence,

Category IV – mySAP Employee Licence and

Category V – mySAP Development Licence to name a few.

Similarly, some software may have Read Only and Transactional Licences. The licence compliance is determined by the financial value of these licences used. In other words, the total financial value of the licences used cannot exceed the total financial value of the licences entitled or purchased.

The SAP Licence position of an organisation is compliant as long as the total financial value of the licences used is less than the total financial value of the licences purchased, provided there is Special Clause in the Licence Agreement. The graph below in *Figure 14.5* is an example of a Financial Reconciliation and Compliance Report for SAP licences.

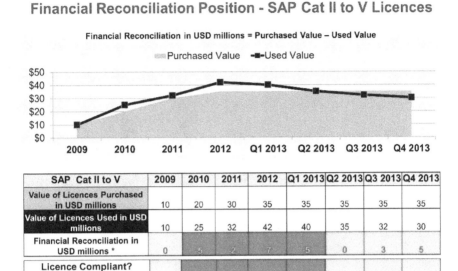

Financial Reconciliation Position - SAP Cat II to V Licences

Financial Reconciliation in USD millions = Purchased Value – Used Value

Purchased Value ▬■▬Used Value

SAP Cat II to V	2009	2010	2011	2012	Q1 2013	Q2 2013	Q3 2013	Q4 2013
Value of Licences Purchased in USD millions	10	20	30	35	35	35	35	35
Value of Licences Used in USD millions	10	25	32	42	40	35	32	30
Financial Reconciliation in USD millions *	0	5	-2	-7	-5	0	3	5
Licence Compliant? (Yes / No)	Yes	No	No	No	No	Yes	Yes	Yes

* Non-compliance is mitigated by Special Clause which states
- Value of licences used shall not exceed value of licences purchased

Figure 14.5: Financial Reconciliation and Compliance Report

Financial Reports

The graphs below are samples of Financial Reports. The first graph in *Figure 14.6* depicts the year on year Investments and Maintenance and Support (M&S) Costs. It also highlights any wastage due to over licensing and savings after optimising licence usage.

YoY Investments, M&S Costs, Wastage and Savings in USD millions

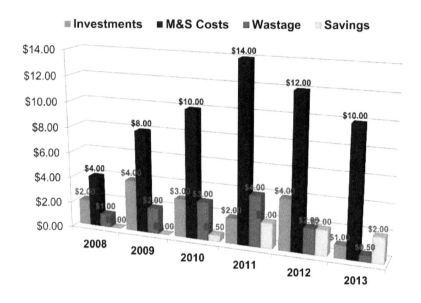

Figure 14.6: Financial Costs Report

The second graph in *Figure 14.7* shows the cost avoidance and savings due to the different pro-active initiatives in Software Licence Management.

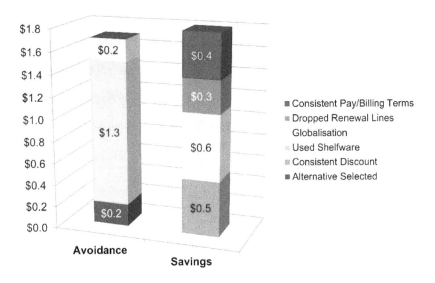

Figure 14.7: Financial Cost Avoidance and Savings Report

Chapter 15: What are the two critical pillars of Software Licence Management Framework?

The 'Governance Model' and 'People, Processes and Tools' collectively are the two critical pillars of Software Licence Management Framework. There would be no credible Software Licence Management Framework without a functioning governance model that engages all key stakeholders across an organisation and its software providers backed up by standard processes and tools.

First Pillar - Governance Model

A robust Governance Model is one of the most important deliverable of Level 3 – 'Defined' stage of the *Licence Optimisation Maturity Model* covered in *Chapter 13*. Governance is a critical element to any successful Framework and Software Licence Management is no exception. This is especially true, since our vision is to provide business value to our value chain partners internally by reducing TCO and to transform our relationship with our software providers into a partnership based on "transparency", trust and mutual benefit.

The governance model also answers the question, *"What is in it for you and me"?* Everyone has a stake in Software Licence Management since each one of us uses at least one software either from a Business or IT perspective and each software requires licence. The stakes grow higher according to your role and the level you are in the governance model.

Remember, we mentioned earlier that the Senior Management like the CIO or CFO or CEO are directly responsible for any breaches and hence have the highest stake.

*The three levels of governance are **Strategic, Tactical** and **Operational** as depicted in the Figure 15.1 below.*

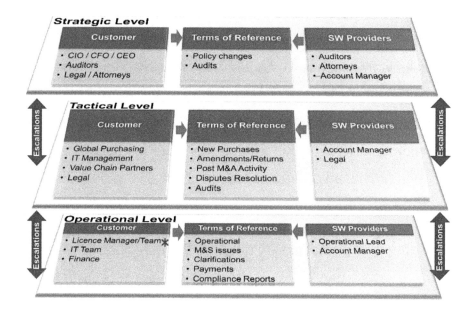

Figure 15.1: First Pillar - Governance Model

Operational Level

At this level, the Licence Manager, IT Team and Finance interact with the Account Manager or Operational Leads of a software provider on day to day operational issues. The Terms of Reference for this forum covers Maintenance & Support (M&S) tasks, seeking clarifications on terms of usage, payments and providing software audit or compliance reports if requested. Any escalation is cascaded to the Tactical level.

Please note that the Licence Management Team, if available is the SPOC – single point of contact for all software providers for any issues with software licensing. Any phishing emails or queries from software providers regarding licences – i.e., number of licences, number of users or any reports should be routed to the Licence Management Team and not handled directly by the business or application support providers.

Tactical Level

At this level, it is imperative for Global Purchasing and IT Management in any organisation to engage with the Account

Manager of a software provider. The Terms of Reference of this forum covers new or additional purchases, return and refund of licences, amendments to agreements, post M&A activities of the customer or their software providers, escalations from the operational level and any resolution of disputes or differences in interpretation of the contract. The Legal department is involved in exceptional cases for legal consultations. They meet when there is an absolute need based on new demands or issues.

Strategic Level

At this level, the Senior Executives, Auditors and Legal Department or Attorneys get involved only when there is a real demand for a software audit and during major policy changes. Any risks of financial exposure are cascaded from the Tactical level to the Strategic level to ensure we have an Audit Strategy in place and an Audit Response Task Team put together to deal with external auditors and Software Providers.

It may be interesting to note that the Account Manager of a software provider is conspicuously missing at the strategic level since he/she no longer forms part of the

Audit team during the audit stage. Hence, there is little impetus for an Account Manager to push for software audits since he/she does not gain any financial benefit or commission from penalties resulting from an audit and he/she will have to grapple with a disgruntled customer after the audit. But, the mere threat of a software audit encourages a customer to buy additional licences to reduce financial exposure and this in turn benefits some over-zealous Account Managers through commissions.

Second Pillar - People, Processes and Tools

The second pillar of the framework is People, Processes and Tools. People, Processes and Tools collectively are one of the most important deliverable of Level 3 – 'Defined' stage of the Licence Optimisation Maturity Model covered in *Chapter 13*.

The Process Flow diagram in *Figure 15.2* below shows a sample high level workflow that is based on the two lifecycles mentioned in the definition of Software Licence Management i.e., Software Ownership Lifecycle and Employee / User Lifecycle covered in *Chapter 2*.

You can identify the key stakeholders that are involved or associated with Software Licence Management Framework and their respective processes in each of those blocks. The key stakeholders are Business, IT Management (IM) and IT Support, Licence Management, Global Purchasing, Legal, Accounts Payable, Finance and the Software Providers.

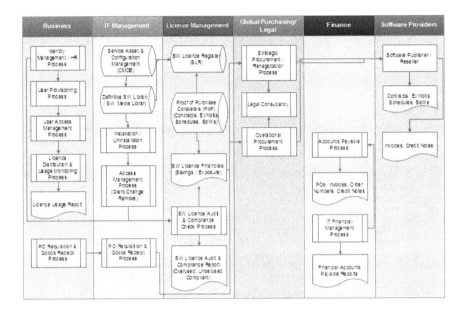

Figure 15.2: Second Pillar - People, Process and Tools

In most organisations, our focus was on the Licence Management block and to define processes that either didn't exist or were at a nascent stage. If you see closely, you can see how the Licence Management processes interface with the existing processes of other key stakeholders. This is also evident in *Figure 15.3* below. The objective is to provide guidelines or licence checkpoints to key stakeholders so that they can incorporate them in their respective processes.

This high level workflow forms the foundation for the detailed processes.

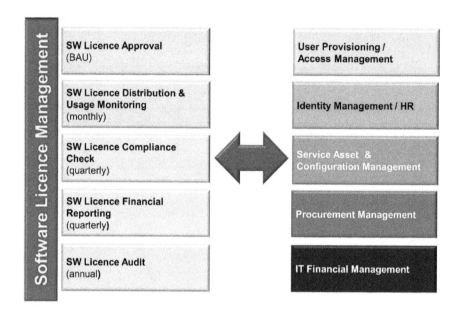

Figure 15.3: Interfaces with other Processes

Figure 15.4 below shows a sample high level software sourcing process.

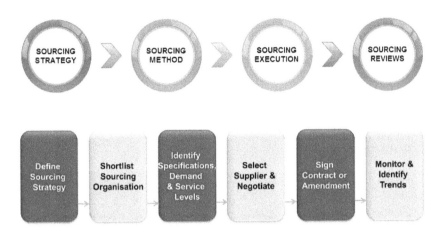

Figure 15.4: Sample Software Sourcing Process

Chapter 16: How can we contribute towards software licence optimisation?

We are saving the best for last, where each employee in an organisation can make a difference by their individual contribution. We may have covered some of the points before.

To summarise,

1. Licence Management Team should be the SPOC for all software licence issues, Hence, it is imperative that the business units, external/ internal application support providers and other value partners do not entertain any phishing emails or queries from software providers and to route them to the Licence Management Team

   a. In some organisations, we learnt about instances where some software providers approached a third party application support provider for user information on the customer organisation and the third party application support provider provided them the customer user numbers. The software provider interpreted them incorrectly and knocked on the customer's doors to question on over utilisation of user licences based on incorrect figures.

b. Remember, it takes just one disgruntled employee or application support provider to be the whistle blower or inadvertently provide incorrect information to the software provider and to trigger a software compliance enquiry.

2. The Business, IT Management and Project Teams should consult the Licence Management Team and Global Purchasing first before they approach the software providers for new software or additional licences. The Licence Management team can first check for availability of the software in the customer organisation's inventory or SLR and if there any spare licences allocate them. If there are no licences or the spare licences are inadequate to meet new demands and if they are absolutely required, the Licence Management Team can engage Global Purchasing to purchase new software or additional licences centrally. Global Purchasing can negotiate a better deal on new software or additional licences if they engage with the software provider first rather than as a follow up to the negotiations between the Business Unit and the software provider.

a. In an organisation, a particular software was purchased from a software provider. Originally, the Business was quoted $300k. Global Purchasing was able to bring this quote down to $40k. When Global Purchasing stated that they had no budget and had only $40k spare, the software provider agreed and provided the software.

3. Business must measure their licence entitlements regularly; every quarter at a minimal and report these numbers to the Licence Management Team. This will ensure we are within the licence threshold or purchased limits.

    a. In SAP, you can run the SAP workload bench every quarter to measure compliance of user type licences. Similarly, it should be rolled out to all software.

Chapter 17: How to handle a demand for Software Audit?

Legally, software providers have the right to audit their customers embedded in the software agreements. Adobe, Microsoft, Oracle, SAP and other large software publishers conduct regular software audits on their customers. Some of them label it mildly as Software Asset Management Review, Software Assessment or Effective Licence Position Assessment instead of the stronger term "Software Audit".

How would you handle a demand for a Software Audit from your software provider? Would you panic or do you have a mechanism in place to respond to such eventualities? If you have a Software Licence Management Framework in place as described in the previous chapters of this book, you will be in a stronger position to deal with any demand for a software audit without any panic. If not, you will have to expedite the process explained in the previous chapters to meet the specific audit request from the software provider.

For starters, the demand for an audit has to come through the right channels from a software provider. This demand has to be sent to the right level of governance in an organisation. It is in the interest of the software provider to demand an audit only after the Account Manager has exhausted all channels to settle any discrepancies.

On receipt of the demand for an audit from a software provider, the Audit Strategy is invoked and an Audit Response Task Team is summoned. This team will involve Senior Leaders or Executives, Legal Department or Attorneys to deal with it at the strategic level of the Governance Model covered in *Chapter 15.*

The team first acknowledges the demand and agrees on a date convenient for the organisation based on the timeframe agreed in the contract. In the interim, the tactical level teams will provide support to evaluate any risks of financial exposure and challenge any unwarranted demands from the software provider conducting the software audit. The Audit Response Task Team will engage with the Auditors of the Software Provider either in-house or externally.

The biggest drawback of a Software Audit is the unbudgeted costs and diversion of essential resources and time from delivery of business as usual and critical projects. It takes time to defend an audit at short notice by collecting the Effective Licensing Position data and Proof of Purchase collaterals.

Chapter 18: How to fend off a Software Audit?

Although software licensing is inevitable, Business and organisations have a few choices to fend off software audits by software providers. Some of the options are

- Avoid right to audit clauses in software agreements altogether or ensure simpler or more automated licensing mechanisms or

- Sign up to an all-inclusive agreement. However, these may lead to excessive supply of software licences compared to actual demands including incremental requirements thereby causing financial wastage or

- Implement a Software Licence Management Framework described in the previous chapters of this book and be prepared for software audit demands at any point in time.

Chapter 19: Conclusion

"Big wheels move on small hinges".

We believe, with the provision of these small hinges and with the help of each licenced user in your organisation, you can achieve Operational and Compliance Readiness and fulfil your vision using the simple strategy of *ORGANISE, ANALYSE and MOBILISE*.

Thank you for reading.

www.ingramcontent.com/pod-product-compliance
Lightning Source LLC
LaVergne TN
LVHW052304060326
832902LV00021B/3702